Garden HEROES

Rufus Bellamy

Published 2009 by
A & C Black Publishers Ltd.
36 Soho Square, London, W1D 3QY
www.acblack.com

ISBN HB 978-1-4081-0861-1
    PB 978-1-4081-1302-8

Series consultant: Gill Matthews

Text copyright © 2009 Rufus Bellamy

This book is produced using paper that is made from wood grown in managed, sustainable forests. It is natural, renewable and recyclable. The logging and manufacturing processes conform to the environmental regulations of the country of origin.

Produced for A & C Black by Calcium.
Printed and bound in China by C&C Offset Printing Co.

All the internet addresses given in this book were correct at the time of going to press. The author and publishers regret any inconvenience caused if addresses have changed or sites have ceased to exist, but can accept no responsibility for any such changes.

Acknowledgements
The publishers would like to thank the following for their kind permission to reproduce their photographs:
Cover: Istockphoto: Dean Murray; Shutterstock. **Pages:** Dreamstime: Thomas Dobner 5t, David Job 17b, Nadezda Pyastolova 19, Nitipong Ballapavanich 2, 4t, 8t, 16t, 18t, Lee Daniels 3, 6, 11b, 22–23, Clayton Hansen 10t, Sandy Manter 8, Pavlo Maydikov 13, Dean Murray 12t, Dieter Spears 20; Shutterstock: Goran Cakmazovic 5b, Peter Clark 17t, Steven Collins 7b, David Davis 11t, Arlene Jean Gee 9b, Lukás Hejtman 15t, Jan van der Hoeven 21b, Iperl 7t, Johnnychaos 9t, Cathy Keifer 21t, Alexey Khromushin 15b, Steve Mann 16, Gyula Matics 12b, Steve McWilliam 18b, Moronsi 4, Gordana Sermek 10b, Juris Sturainis 14.

Contents

Garden Heroes

Gardens, backyards, parks, and even school grounds are full of amazing animals and plants doing amazing things. In this book you'll get to meet some of the wildlife "action heroes" that live near your home. You'll discover just what they're up to and find out why they are so important.

Wildlife homes

Hedgehogs have a habit of burrowing in piles of leaves or bonfires. So be careful not to disturb them.

Gardens, and the other open spaces around people's houses, are really important for wildlife. They provide places where plants can grow and where animals can make a home and find food. Many animals and plants are threatened. This makes it important that gardens are wildlife friendly. If your garden is large enough, leave an overgrown wild area – small creatures will soon move in.

Nature note

Feeding birds is one way in which people can help wildlife. This is important when the weather is cold and food is in short supply.

Lovely ladybirds

Ladybirds eat pests, such as aphids, that attack garden plants. In the winter, these spotted garden heroes often sleep bunched together in little groups.

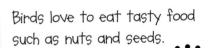

Birds love to eat tasty food such as nuts and seeds.

Ladybirds are a garden's best friend.

Green Food

From the leaves on the trees to the grass on the lawn, gardens are full of greenery. All these green plants can do something amazing. They can make their own food.

Green plants use energy from the sun to turn water and a gas called **carbon dioxide** into a type of sugar. They use this as food so they can live and grow. Carbon dioxide gets into a plant's leaves from the air. Water is taken in from the soil by its **roots**.

Precious plants

Animals can't make their own food. They eat plants, or they eat animals that eat plants. This means that all animals, including people, rely on green plants to survive.

Nature note

Trees have to lift water all the way up to their leaves. A big tree, such as an oak, can drink enough water in a day to fill a large bath.

Green plants and trees are the real garden heroes.

Some leaves become red and yellow in the autumn, others change from green to brown.

Colour changes

Green plants are green because they have a chemical called **chlorophyll** in their leaves. Chlorophyll lets them capture the energy of the sun. In the autumn, leaves change colour as their chlorophyll disappears.

Marvellous Munchers

Garden plants are a feast for many animals. Slugs eat lettuces and rabbits nibble grass, while birds peck the seeds, fruit, and berries from all sorts of flowers, shrubs, and trees.

Animals that only eat plants, such as rabbits, are called herbivores.

Important eaters

When an animal eats a plant's berries or fruit it can be a good thing. They contain seeds from which new plants grow. Many animals help spread out the seeds as they eat, move around, or when they do a poo.

Nature note

Squirrels eat nuts such as acorns (from oak trees). They use their sharp teeth to break open the shells. In autumn, they collect nuts and store them in holes. They dig the nuts up again when food is scarce.

Amazing aphids

Aphids are a real pest in the garden because they eat garden plants, such as roses. But aphids have an amazing secret. They produce something called honeydew. This is sweet and is eaten by many insects and other animals.

Butterflies lay their eggs on plants so the caterpillars that hatch from the eggs can eat them.

Hungry Hunters

The world outside your window is full of hungry hunters. Bluetits work very hard to hunt caterpillars for their chicks. These baby birds can eat over a hundred caterpillars in a day! Hedgehogs spend a lot of time hunting for insects, slugs, snails, and worms.

An owl's excellent eyesight can help it to hunt in the dark.

Nature note

Spiders are amazing hunters. They make super-strong spider silk in their bodies and use it to spin webs to trap flies.

Expert hunters

Many animals have skills that make them good hunters, such as a strong sense of smell or excellent hearing. The song thrush has a very special skill – it can break open snail shells on rocks to get at the animal inside.

Animals that eat other animals are called predators. The animals they catch are called prey.

This moth is hard to see because it looks like the bark of the tree it is sitting on.

Hunting heroes

If there were no predators, the animals they eat would become too numerous. That's why gardeners love ladybirds, lacewings, and hoverflies. They help keep down the number of garden pests. Some animals have markings which frighten hunters away. Others have patterns and colours that make it difficult for hunters to see them. We say they are camouflaged.

Important Insects

On a warm summer's day the air outside is full of action. Bees and other insects buzz about looking for food. Many are searching for the sweet **nectar** and powdery **pollen** that is found inside flowers.

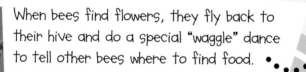

When bees find flowers, they fly back to their hive and do a special "waggle" dance to tell other bees where to find food.

Flowers need insects

When an insect goes inside a flower to look for food, pollen rubs off onto its body. As it flies about, the insect carries this pollen to other flowers.

If the insect passes pollen between two flowers of the same type, an amazing thing can happen: the flowers can start to make seeds from which new plants can grow. That's one reason why insects are real garden heroes. Insects are so important, many gardeners try to attract them by planting flowers that provide nectar.

Butterflies love plants such as buddleias. That's why buddleias are known as the butterfly bush.

Nature note

Many flowers have patterns on their petals that only insects can see. The patterns attract insects. Insects can see these patterns because their eyes can see different types of light to ours.

Amazing Movers

You often only see the animals that live near your home when they move. They could be in search of food, escaping from a predator, or looking for a **mate**. Some amazing movers live in gardens.

Mega movers

A mole could tunnel about half way across a football pitch in just one day! Snails and slugs don't have any legs, but can crawl up walls. They produce a sticky slime that lets them do this. It's this slime that makes the trails they leave behind. Bats are also amazing movers. They fly at night and catch tiny fast-moving insects in the dark.

Snails are amazing climbers! This snail is travelling up a steep plant stem.

The wings of insects such as the hoverfly have to beat up to 300 times per second to make it fly.

A frog can jump over ten times its own body length.

Flying movers

Probably the best movers in a garden are birds. Many of these birds fly thousands of miles in search of food and a place to have babies. For example, swallows fly from Africa to Britain and back again each year. This type of movement is called **migration**.

Nature note

You can see where animals have moved by looking for their prints or tracks. These can usually be found in soft earth.

Heroic Homemakers

Many garden animals make amazing homes. House martins and swallows build nests made of mud. Mice, rabbits, and badgers are just some of the animals that dig to make homes underground.

A wildlife-friendly garden

Because wild animals like their homes to be hidden away, long grass and other "untidy" bits of garden (such as thick hedges and nettle patches) are important. They provide shelter for animals.

Untidy garden corners make good homes for many garden animals.

Trees, such as the oak, are also important homes for many animals and plants. **Fungi** live among their roots and squirrels build nests (called "drays") in their branches.

Plants are also clever at making themselves at home in a garden. Some tough plants, such as the dandelion, are able to grow in cracks in pathways.

A winter sleep

Some garden animals such as hedgehogs **hibernate** during the winter. This is like going into a very deep sleep. They curl up and make themselves a cosy nest in dead leaves.

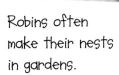

Robins often make their nests in gardens.

Nature note

The area where an animal lives is called its **territory**. Many animals, such as robins, will fight each other to guard their territories.

Radical Recyclers

It's not just people who recycle waste so that it can be used again. In a back garden there are many recycling heroes.

These recyclers feed on dead and decaying plants and animals. They break these things down and release the **nutrients** they contain into the soil. Plants then use these nutrients to live and grow.

Invisible workers

Microscopic bacteria do a lot of this work. Mushrooms and other fungi break down old leaves and other plant material.

Woodlice are just one of many minibeasts that eat rotting plant material.

Wonderful worms

Worms are very important waste recyclers. They eat soil and dead and decaying plants. Worms produce **casts** that are full of nutrients and good for plants. Worms also mix up the soil, which is another way in which they help gardeners.

Nature note

The average garden will have over 10,000 worms living in its soil.

When you see a mushroom you are only seeing a small part of it. The rest of it is made up of a web of tiny fibres that spread out in the soil underneath it.

Extraordinary Offspring

Garden activity is perhaps at its most exciting when a new animal (offspring) arrives. When they are born, animals such as birds, mice, and rabbits are fed and cared for by their parents. But many minibeasts, and other animals such as frogs and toads, must look after themselves.

Finding a mate

To have babies most animals must first attract a mate. They do this in many different ways. For example many birds sing, while grasshoppers make a chirping noise by rubbing their wings against their back legs.

When baby animals are born, they are at risk from predators.

Pupa

Butterfly

When a caterpillar changes into a butterfly, the change is called **metamorphosis**.

Growing and changing

Some animals change a lot as they grow. For example, butterflies lay eggs that hatch into caterpillars. Each caterpillar eats a lot of food, grows, and then forms a pupa (or chrysalis). An amazing change then occurs – the caterpillar becomes a beautiful butterfly.

Nature note

The cuckoo lays its eggs in a nest belonging to another pair of birds. They have to do the hard work of bringing up the baby cuckoo.

Frogs hatch from frogspawn as tiny tadpoles. Over the next few months they grow legs and arms and lose their tails to become adults.

Glossary

carbon dioxide a gas found in air

casts small pile of soil produced by an earthworm

chlorophyll a green pigment found in leaves

fungi mushrooms and some moulds are among the many types of fungi

hibernate to save energy and survive the winter by going into a deep sleep.

mate one of a pair of animals of the same species (one male, one female) that get together to have offspring (babies)

metamorphosis the process by which an animal changes shape as it develops and grows

microscopic too small to be seen with just the eye

migration the large-scale movement of animals in search of food, a place to breed, or warmer weather

nectar a sugary liquid plants make to attract insects

nutrients chemicals plants and animals need to survive

pollen a powder made by the male parts of some plants

roots plant parts that absorb water and nutrients

territory area an animal occupies and defends

Further Information

Websites

Find out how to encourage birds, animals, and insects into your garden at:

www.wildchicken.com/nature/garden/wild000_ wildlife_gardening_for_children.htm

Read a virtual garden wildlife diary at:

www.wildlifewatch.org.uk/wildlifediary

Books

All About Garden Wildlife by David Chandler. New Holland (2008).

In the Garden (Look What I Found!). Franklin Watts (2007).

Microscopic Life in the Garden by Brian Ward. Franklin Watts (2007).

Index